Happy Day!
Things to Make and Do

Written by Judith Conaway
Illustrated by Renzo Barto

Troll Associates

Library of Congress Cataloging in Publication Data

Conaway, Judith (date)
    Happy day!

    Summary: Instructions for making a variety of toys
and games from easily available materials. Includes such
items as a pillowball, juice-can marimba and
tambourine, and a table playhouse.
    1. Handicraft—Juvenile literature.   [1. Handicraft]
I. Barto, Renzo, ill.   II. Title.
TT160.C653   1987   745.5   86-7131
    ISBN 0-8167-0842-8 (lib. bdg.)
    ISBN 0-8167-0843-6 (pbk.)

CONTENTS

Pillowball 4

The Glove Bug 6

Manilanimals 8

Wooden Clothespin People 12

Rhonda the Robot 14

Cup and Tube Flip Game 18

String and Cup Race 20

Table Playhouse 22

The Tube Game 24

Rubber Band-Jo 26

Juice-Can Marimba and Tambourine 30

Personalized Polka Dots 34

Trailing Vine Stamp 38

Socko, The Snake 40

Bagman Toss 42

Animal Raceway 44

PILLOWBALL

Need a soft, quiet indoor sport? Sock it to 'em with a pillowball. You can make one in minutes and have hours of fun!

Here's what you need:

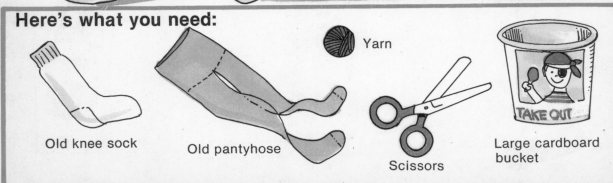

Old knee sock

Old pantyhose

Yarn

Scissors

Large cardboard bucket

TAKE OUT

Here's what you do:

1 Cut the sock off at the ankle. Cut the knit top off the sock, too.

2 Cut the legs off the pantyhose.

3 Tie one end of the sock with yarn. Turn the sock inside out, so that the knot is inside.

4 Wind the pantyhose legs into a ball. Stuff the ball inside the sock. Tie the other end of the sock with yarn.

5 Here are some ways to play with your pillowball: Bat it back and forth as if it were a volleyball. Or, cut the bottom out of a large cardboard bucket. Make a hole near the top and thread some yarn through it. Hang up the basket and play pillow basketball.

THE GLOVE BUG

You've got to hand it to this creature! It's weird. It's lovable. And it's easy to make.

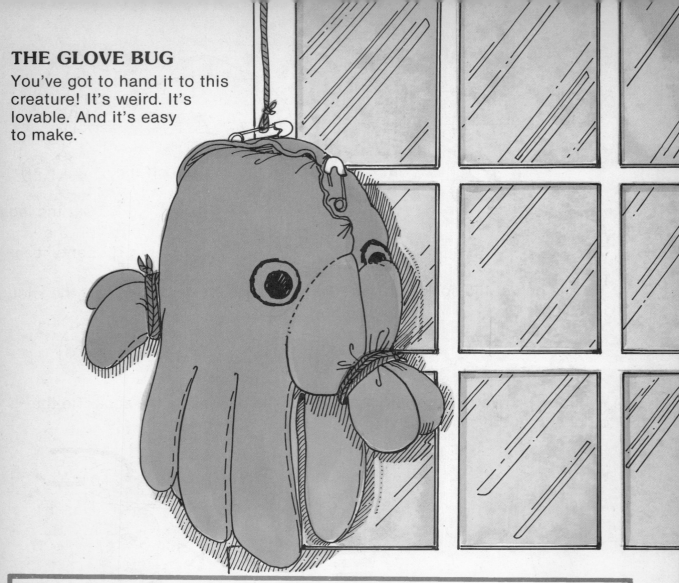

Here's what you need:

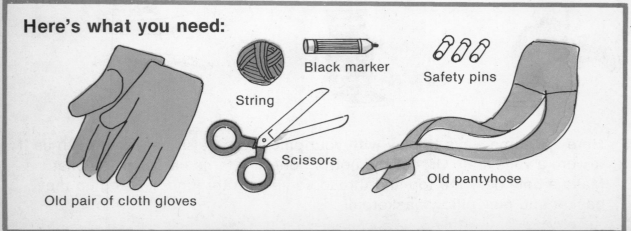

Old pair of cloth gloves

String

Black marker

Scissors

Safety pins

Old pantyhose

Here's what you do:

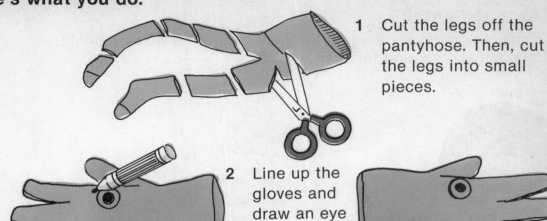

1 Cut the legs off the pantyhose. Then, cut the legs into small pieces.

2 Line up the gloves and draw an eye on each one as shown.

3 Use the pantyhose to stuff the thumbs and pinky fingers, but not the other fingers of the gloves. Then, stuff the palms.

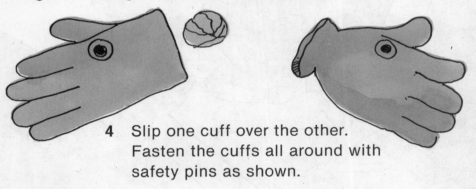

4 Slip one cuff over the other. Fasten the cuffs all around with safety pins as shown.

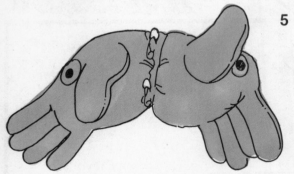

5 Tie the two pinky fingers together to make the bug's tail. Tie the two thumbs together to make the bug's antennae. The other fingers hang loose to make the bug's legs.

6 Tie a length of string to one of the safety pins. Now hang up your glove bug!

MANILANIMALS

Old manila envelopes are just the right weight for making miniature animals. Why not make enough for a whole zoo?

Here's what you need:

Manila envelopes

Scissors

Glue

Pencil

crayons

Crayons

Here's what you do:

1 Copy the animal shapes from the following pages. Position the backbone of each animal along the folded edge of the envelope.

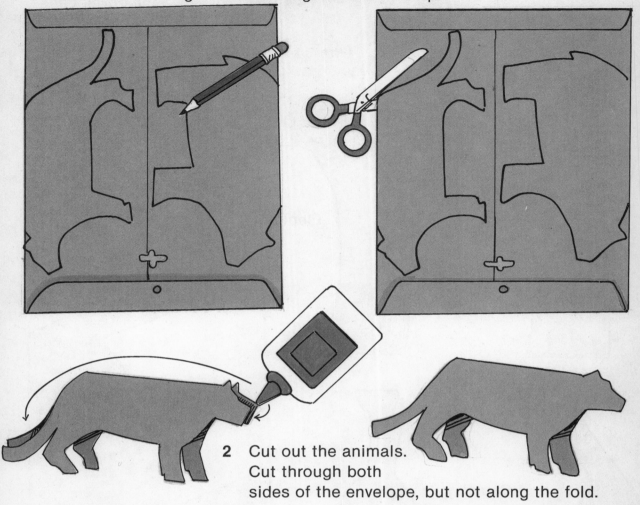

2 Cut out the animals. Cut through both sides of the envelope, but not along the fold.

3 Put small spots of glue inside the envelope near the animal's face and tail. Press the two sides together.

4 You can draw faces, fur, and stripes on your animals. Be sure to draw on both sides.

5 Stand the animals by spreading the legs about 1″ apart.

Note: The seal folds a little differently. Glue the seal's face and back flipper. Allow it to dry. Spread the two front flippers. Bend the rear flipper to one side.

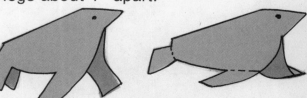

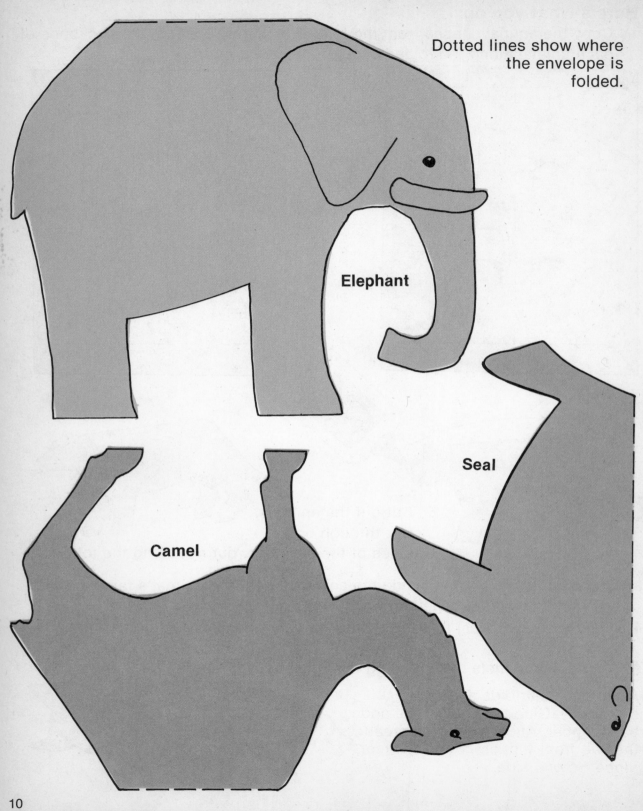

Dotted lines show where the envelope is folded.

Elephant

Seal

Camel

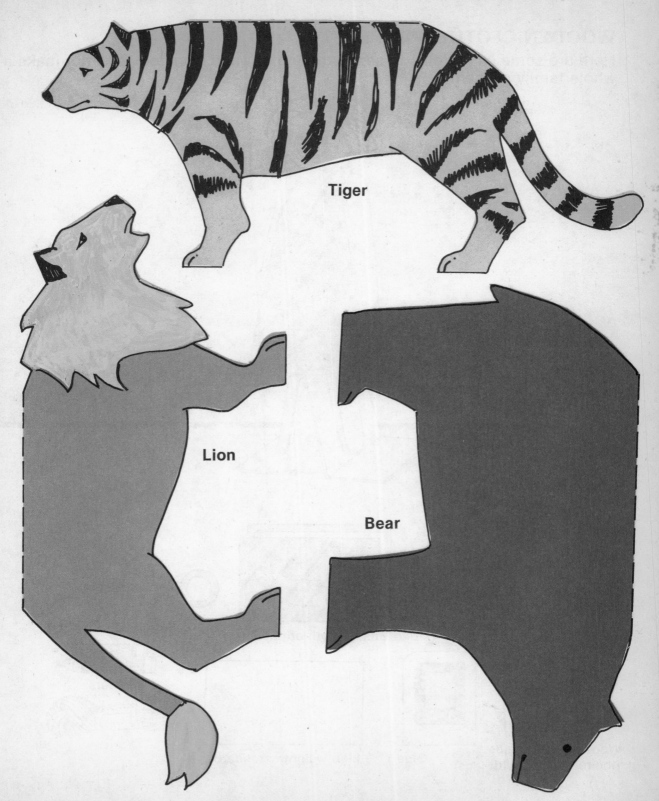

Tiger

Lion

Bear

WOODEN CLOTHESPIN PEOPLE

Here are some small folks to send strolling through your zoo. Why not make a whole family of them?

Here's what you need:

Pencil

Ruler

Wooden clothespins
(the round kind with legs)

Glue

Lightweight cardboard

Bits of cloth or paper

Scissors

Markers

Yarn

Here's what you do:

1 Draw a face on the clothespin with markers.

2 Glue bits of yarn for hair.

3 For the dress, cut out this pattern from a piece of colored paper or cloth.

4 Use these patterns to cut the arms from cardboard.

5 Wrap the dress around the clothespin and glue in place. Glue the arms to the sides of the dress.

6 Cut a strip of 1-½″ × 4″ cardboard for the stand. Make a fold at each inch, lengthwise. Then, fold as shown.

Position the legs of the clothespin over the stand.

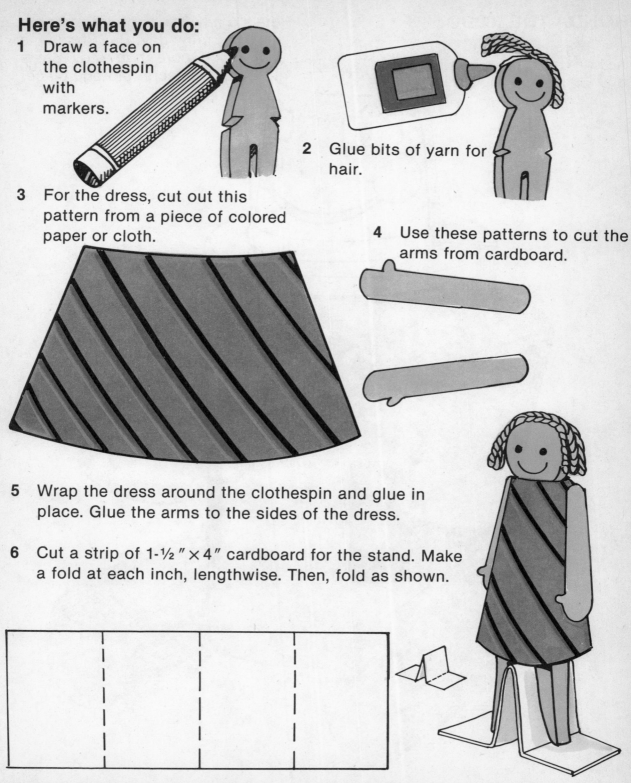

RHONDA THE ROBOT

Here's a new toy to cheer you on a rainy day. But Rhonda is much more than a toy. She's also a secret storage place!

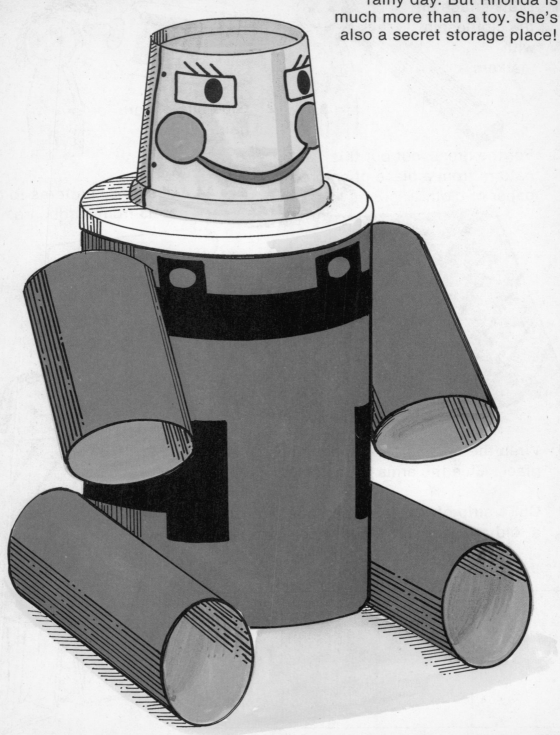

Here's what you need:

Empty oatmeal container

4 Toilet-tissue tubes

Paper fasteners

Scissors

Empty yogurt container

Newspaper

Nail

Paint and brush

Here's what you do:

1 Remove the lids of the oatmeal and yogurt containers. Place the 2 lids together so that they are touching each other as shown.

2 To fasten them, use the nail to make a hole in each lid. Then, push a paper fastener through both holes and bend the points down.

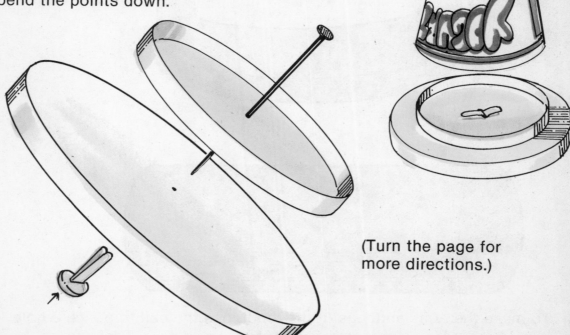

(Turn the page for more directions.)

3 Use the nail to punch 4 holes in the oatmeal carton, 2 on each side. The holes should be directly opposite each other.

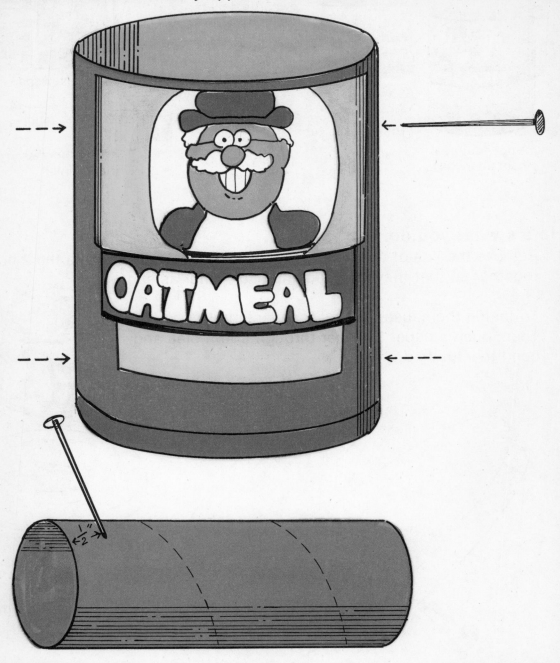

4 To make the arms and legs of the robot, use the nail to punch a hole ½″ away from the end of each toilet-tissue tube.

5 Use paper fasteners to connect the arms and legs to the body.

6 To complete Rhonda, just put the oatmeal lid onto the oatmeal container with the yogurt lid facing up. Attach the yogurt container as shown.

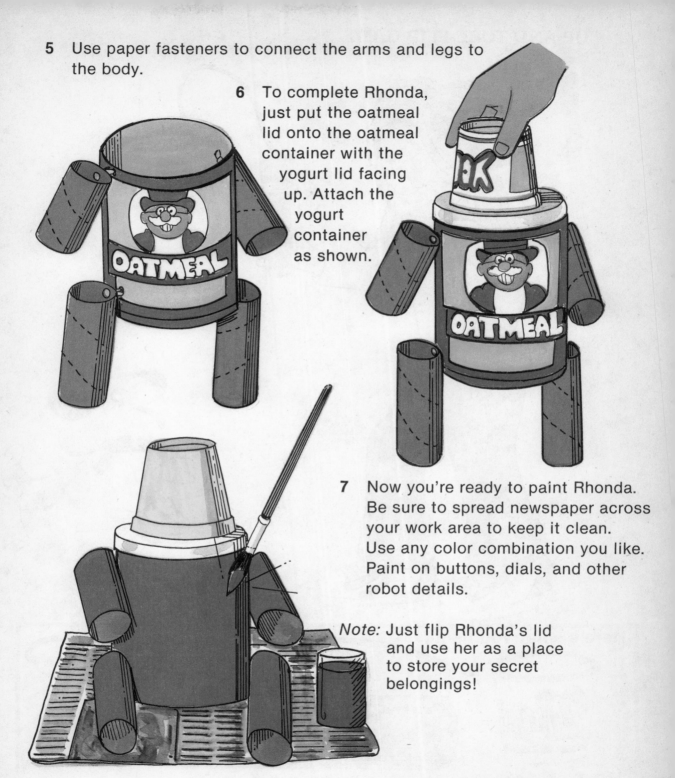

7 Now you're ready to paint Rhonda. Be sure to spread newspaper across your work area to keep it clean. Use any color combination you like. Paint on buttons, dials, and other robot details.

Note: Just flip Rhonda's lid and use her as a place to store your secret belongings!

CUP AND TUBE FLIP GAME

Here's what you need:

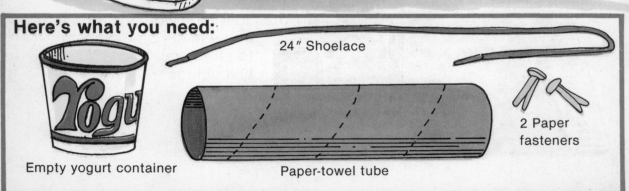

24" Shoelace

Empty yogurt container

Paper-towel tube

2 Paper fasteners

Here's what you do:

1 Use the points of a paper fastener to punch a hole in the bottom center of the yogurt carton.

2 Tie one end of the shoelace to the fastener as shown. Then, push the paper fastener through the hole and bend the points down.

3 Tie the other end of the shoelace to another paper fastener as shown. Use that fastener to punch a hole 1″ from the end of the paper-towel tube. Then, push the paper fastener through the hole and bend the points down to secure it in place.

4 To play the game, position the tube so that the fastener is at the top. Hold the bottom of the tube. See if you can flip the string so that the cup lands on the tube.

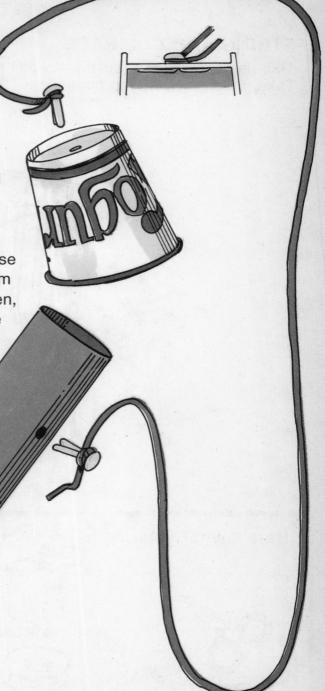

STRING AND CUP RACE

This game is easy to make and easy to play. But it's not so easy to win. Take the string and cup challenge!

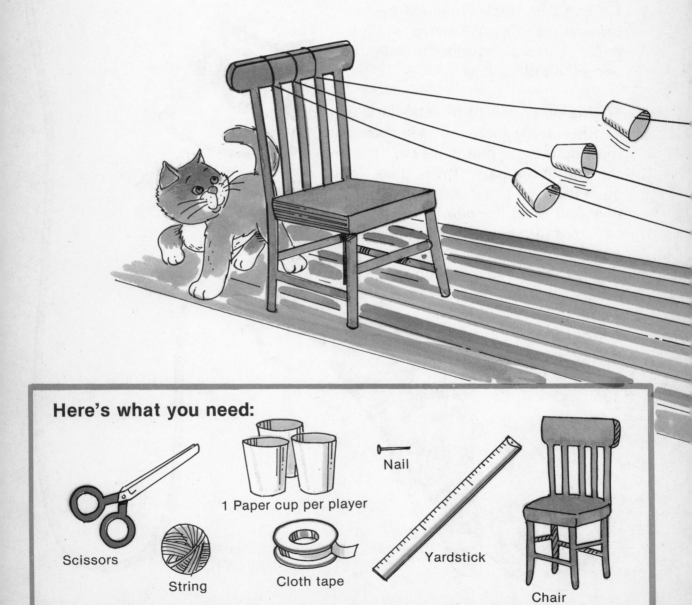

Here's what you need:

Scissors

String

1 Paper cup per player

Cloth tape

Nail

Yardstick

Chair

Here's what you do:

1 Use the nail to make a hole in the bottom center of each paper cup.

2 Place a chair at one end of the playing area. Measure the distance to the other end of the playing area. Then, mark a starting line about 3 feet in from the end with cloth tape.

3 Cut a piece of string for each player. Each piece should be exactly 5 feet longer than the length of the playing area.

4 Tie one end of the string to the chair as shown. Thread a paper cup through each string, so that the bottoms face the chair.

To race, slide all cups so they touch the chair. Each player stands behind the starting line, holding a string. At the signal, players must try to make their cups slide down the string. The first player whose cup passes the finish line wins. *Note:* Players may not touch another player's cup or string.

TABLE PLAYHOUSE

Here's what you need:

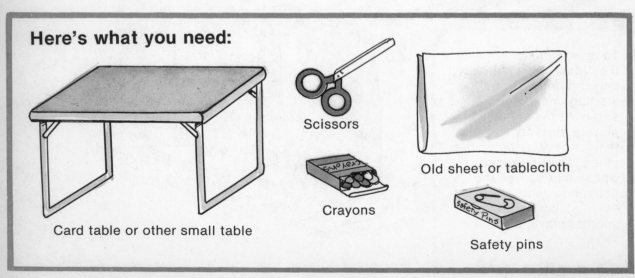

Card table or other small table

Scissors

Crayons

Old sheet or tablecloth

Safety pins

Here's what you do:

1 Drape an old sheet or tablecloth over a table. Be sure that the sheet hangs evenly over the table. The sheet should be long enough to just about reach the floor. (If the sheet is too long, trim it all around.)

2 Use a crayon to mark the places where the sheet touches the 4 corners of the table. Remove the sheet from the table and spread it out on the floor.

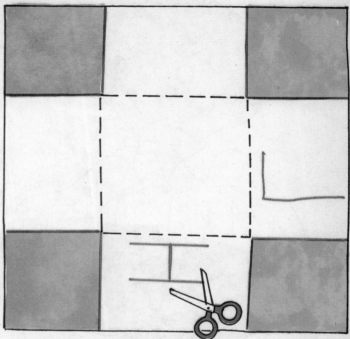

3 Starting at each crayon mark, draw 2 straight lines to the end of the sheet as shown. You will have 4 squares, one in each corner of the sheet. Cut the 4 squares. When you finish, your sheet will look like a large cross.

4 To make the window and door, draw an H and a backwards L on the sheet as shown. Cut along the lines of the H to make the window. Cut along the lines of the L to make the door.

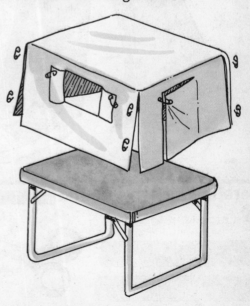

5 Now drape your house over the table. Use safety pins to fasten the window shutters and the door.

6 Use crayons to decorate the outside of your house.

THE TUBE GAME

Here's a game that will have you and your friends going around in circles!

Here's what you need:

- Large Marble
- Markers
- 2 Paper-towel tubes
- Scissors
- Glue
- Corrugated cardboard

WHO AM I?

1. I was a very rich man.

2. God told me to look for a city.

3. God told me that I would be the father of many nations.

4. God told me to sacrifice my son, Isaac, upon an altar.

ABRAHAM   O.T.

Here's what you do:

1 Cut a large circle or oval shape out of cardboard.

2 Draw another circle in the center of the large one. Mark this circle "Start."

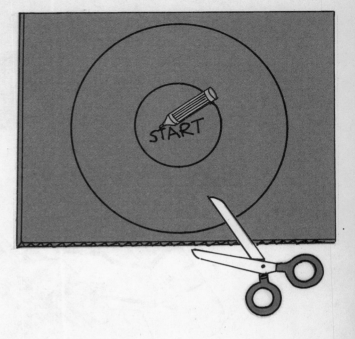

3 Cut the 2 paper-towel tubes into smaller sections.
Cut one into 4 parts...

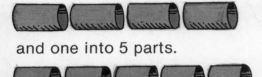

and one into 5 parts.

4 Write the number 10 on each of the large tubes and 5 on each of the small ones.

5 Glue the tube sections to the cardboard as shown. Hold each tube down until the glue starts to dry.

6 To play the game, hold the board in front of you like a tray. Place the marble in the middle. Now tilt the board so the marble rolls. The object of the game is to roll the ball through as many tubes as possible. Your turn ends when the marble falls off the board. You get the number of points that appears on each tube you rolled through. How high is your score?

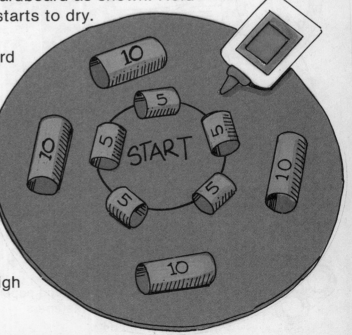

RUBBER BAND-JO

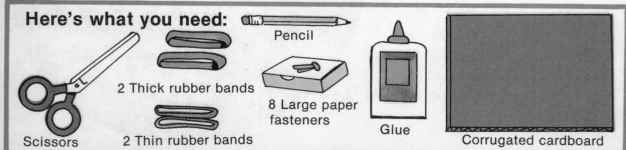

Here's what you need:

Pencil

Scissors

2 Thick rubber bands

2 Thin rubber bands

8 Large paper fasteners

Glue

Corrugated cardboard

26

Here's what you do:

1 Copy the banjo pattern shown on the following pages onto a piece of cardboard. Cut out 2 of these shapes.

2 Cut a center hole in each piece. Be sure to cut in from the edges and start the cuts at opposite sides of each piece.

3 Glue the 2 pieces together as shown. Use lots of glue!

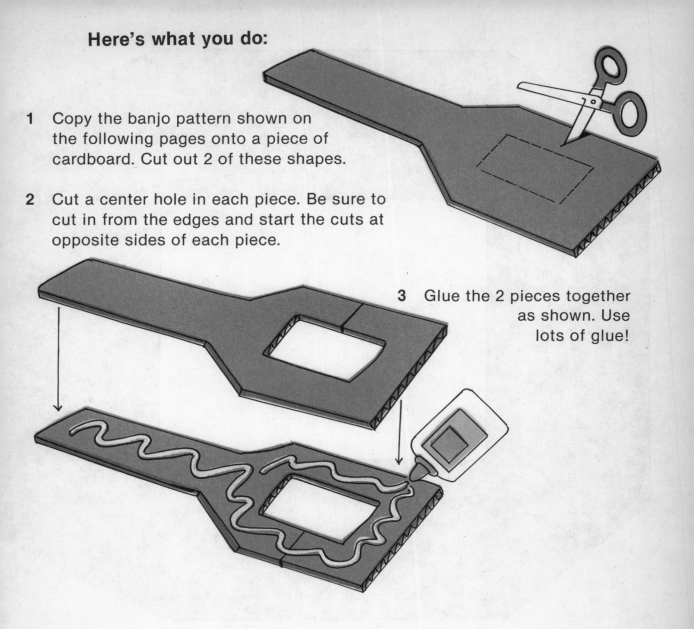

(Turn the page for more directions.)

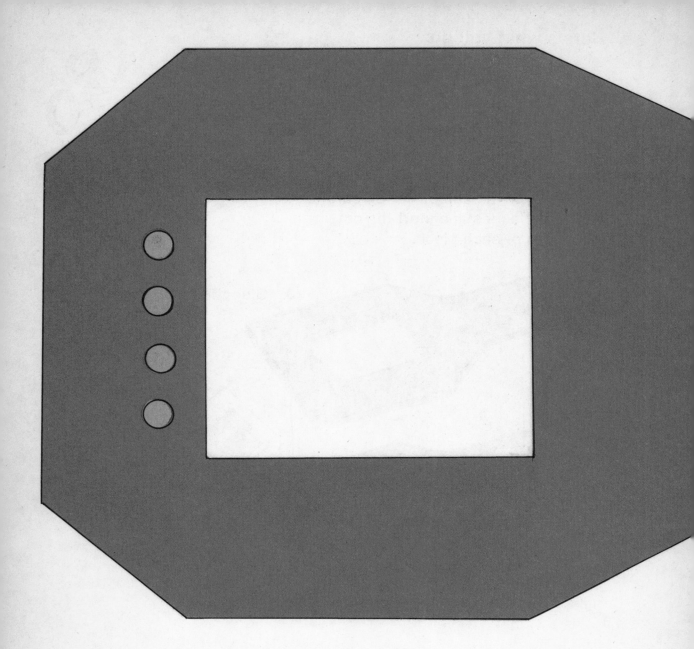

4 Make 8 holes with the paper fastener: 4 along the top and 4 on the bottom as shown. Insert a fastener in each hole. Be sure the heads are all facing the same side. Bend all points down flat.

5 Stretch the rubber bands between the fasteners, across the open area of the banjo. Loop the ends over the heads of the fasteners.

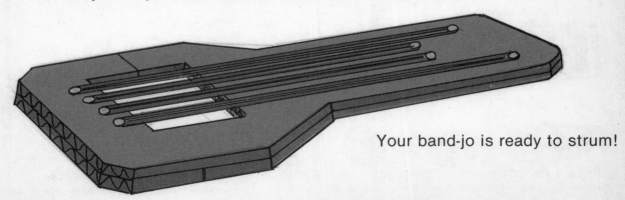

Your band-jo is ready to strum!

JUICE-CAN MARIMBA AND TAMBOURINE

Here's what you need:

3 Small juice cans

Coin

3 Large juice cans

2 Aluminum pie plates

Scissors

Ruler

8 Paper fasteners

Heavy yarn

yarn

Hole puncher

Metal washers

Pebbles

Here's what you do to make the marimba:

1 Cut the open ends of the cardboard cans as shown. Be sure to leave the metal top on each one. Cut each can at an angle, making each one a little shorter than the one before it.

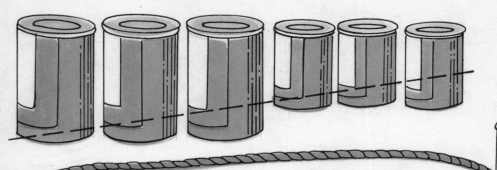

2 Use the points of a paper fastener to make holes, one on each side of each can. The holes should be about ½" down from the metal lid and opposite each other.

3 Fasten the cans together, in order, from the longest to the shortest. Insert the paper fasteners as shown. Be sure you have a paper fastener in the outer holes of the first and last cans.

4 Cut a piece of yarn about 2-½ feet long. Tie the ends to the fasteners on the outer cans.

5 To play the marimba, hang the yarn around your neck. Tap on the metal tops of the cans. Use your fingers to tap. Or, make a heavy metal sound by using a coin.

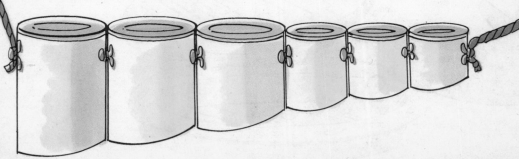

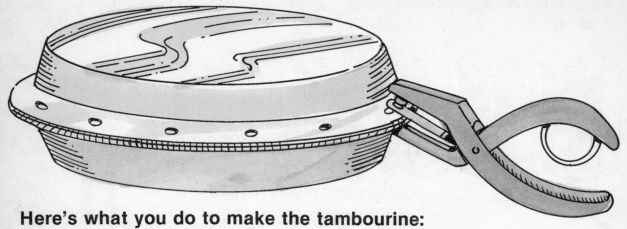

Here's what you do to make the tambourine:

1 Place two aluminum pie plates together as shown. Punch holes around the edges of both plates. (To keep the holes lined up, slip a short length of yarn through the last two holes you make.)

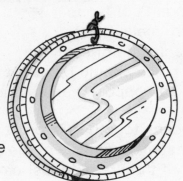

2 Place a handful of pebbles into the pie plate and cover it with the other plate.

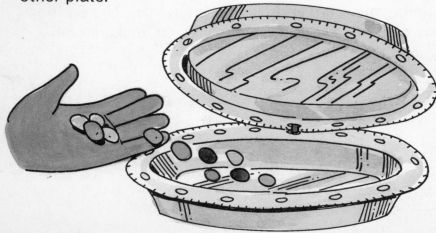

3 Weave some yarn through the pairs of holes and tie a strong knot at the end.

4 Attach metal washers to the plates with small pieces of yarn as shown.

You're ready to shake!

PERSONALIZED POLKA DOTS

You can have more than a spot of fun with these quick stencils. Make your own stationery, wrapping paper, or cards.

Here's what you need:

Hole puncher

Tape

Index cards

Paper

Scissors

Pencil

Paints and brush or markers

Ruler

Here's what you do:

1 Cut rectangles from index cards. Cut to the size shown on the following pages.

2 Print your initials on the rectangles.

3 Punch holes along the lines of your letters, using a hole puncher.

4 Tape the cards together with tiny bits of tape.

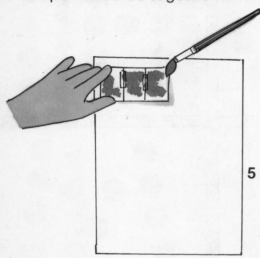

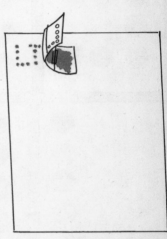

5 Place the cards at the top of a sheet of paper. Go over the holes with paints or markers. Wait a few seconds for the paint to dry. Then lift off the cards. Your monogram will be printed in polka dots.

6 You can use this same idea to spell messages or make other pictures. Just be sure the rectangles you use are small enough so that the hole puncher can reach properly to form your lines.

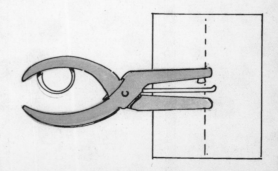

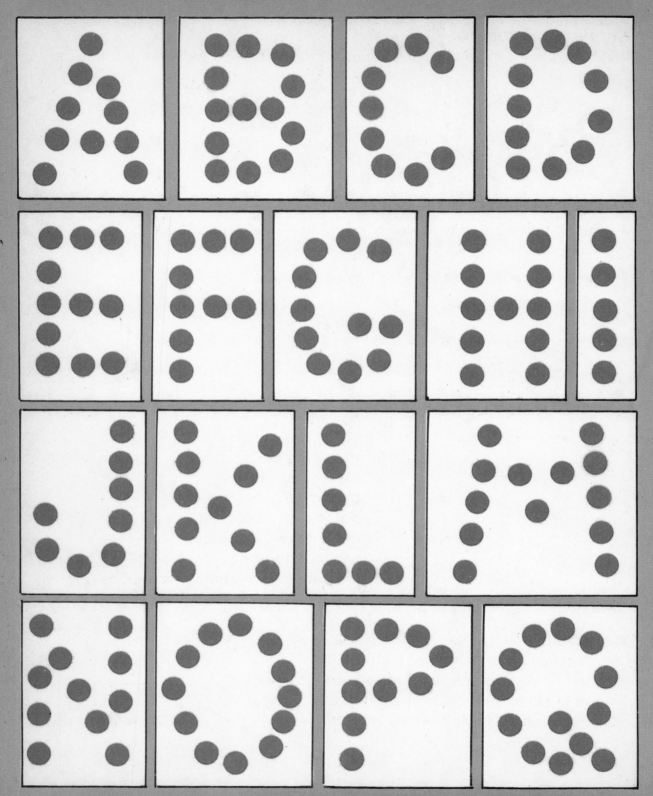

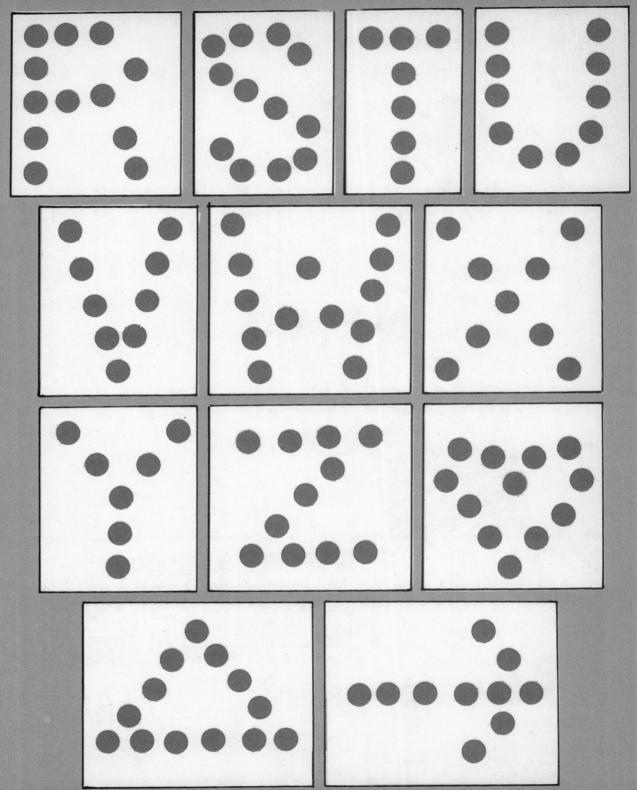

TRAILING VINE STAMP

Here's a quick way to print a design! Just repeat the leaf pattern. Then add vines to connect the leaves.

Here's what you need:

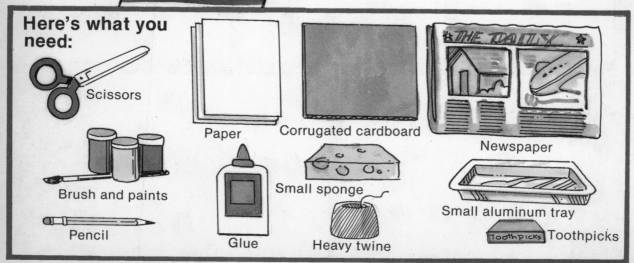

Scissors

Paper

Corrugated cardboard

Newspaper

Brush and paints

Small sponge

Small aluminum tray

Pencil

Glue

Heavy twine

Toothpicks

Here's what you do:

1 To make the stamp, cut out a small rectangle of cardboard. Cut 1 rectangle for each leaf design you wish to make.

2 Spread newspaper over the area where you will be working. Apply glue over the surface of the cardboard. Place twine onto the wet glue. Arrange the twine to form a leaf design. Use the toothpick to adjust the twine. Allow the glue to dry completely.

3 To make the stamp pad, place the sponge in the aluminum tray. Coat the surface of the sponge with paint. Let it soak into the sponge completely.

4 Hold the stamp above the sponge, with the leaf design facing down. Press the stamp gently onto the sponge. Hold it down for a few seconds. Then, carefully place the stamp onto the paper you want to decorate. Press down firmly and don't move the stamp around. Gently lift the stamp from the paper.

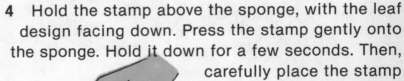

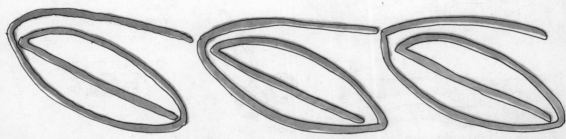

5 Stamp the leaves in a border across the page or from top to bottom. When the paint is dry, draw vine lines to connect the leaves.

SOCKO, THE SNAKE

What do you do with mismatched old socks? You make a toy! But Socko is more than a toy—it's an energy saver, too.

Here's what you need:

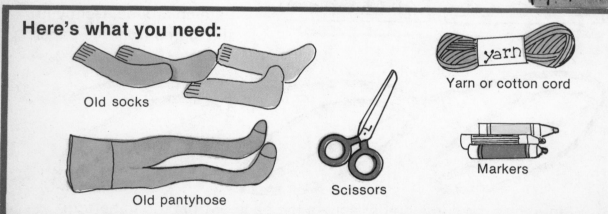

Old socks

Old pantyhose

Scissors

Yarn or cotton cord

Markers

Here's what you do:

1   Cut off the socks at the ankles. Cut the legs from the pantyhose, and cut them into smaller pieces.

2   Tie one of the socks just below the knit top. To tie, wrap the yarn around several times as tightly as you can. Then, tie a double knot.

3   Turn the sock inside out so that the knot is on the inside. You now have the head of your snake.

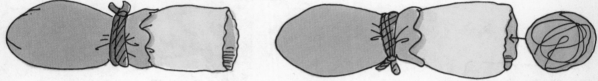

4   Stuff the head with the stockings. Leave about 3″ unstuffed at the end.

5   Slip the knit top of another sock over the open end of the snake's head. Be sure that the ribbing goes at least 3″ over the end. Now wrap and tie where the socks overlap.

6   Stuff the second sock with more stockings. Slip a third sock on. Tie the socks just as you did for the snake's head. Continue until your snake is as long as you want it.

7   If you like, you can draw a face on Socko and add snake markings to the body.

Socko is a serious energy saver! Use Socko to block the cold drafts that come in under doors and windows.

BAGMAN TOSS

Here's what you need:

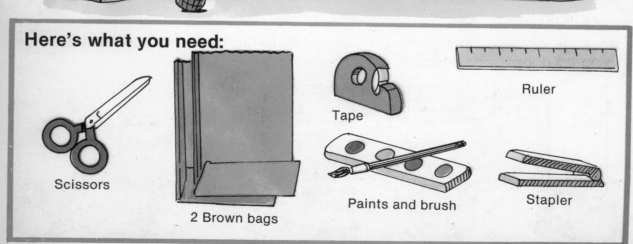

Scissors

2 Brown bags

Tape

Paints and brush

Ruler

Stapler

Here's what you do:

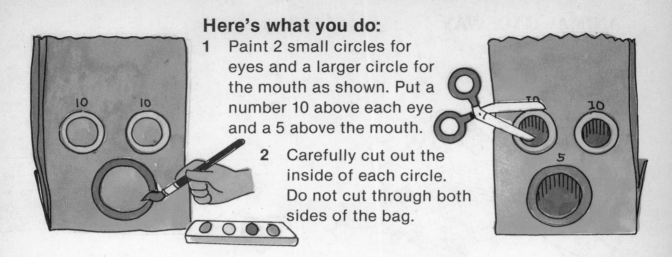

1 Paint 2 small circles for eyes and a larger circle for the mouth as shown. Put a number 10 above each eye and a 5 above the mouth.

2 Carefully cut out the inside of each circle. Do not cut through both sides of the bag.

3 Fold the top of the bag about 1″ down from the top...then fold again. Staple along the fold as shown.

4 To make the balls, cut the other bag into thin strips about ½″ wide. Roll the strips into loose balls. Round off the balls by wrapping with tape. Be sure to keep the balls small enough to fit through the openings. Make at least 5 balls.

5 To play, gently poke the sides of the bag so that it will sit up squarely on a table or the floor. Stand about 2 to 3 feet from the bag and start tossing the paper balls into the openings. Take turns. The one who scores the most points is the winner.

ANIMAL RACEWAY

Here's what you need:

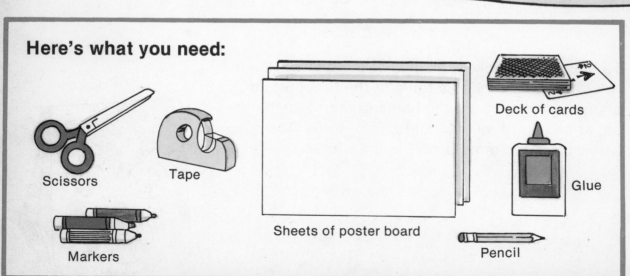

Scissors

Tape

Sheets of poster board

Deck of cards

Glue

Markers

Pencil

Here's what you do:

1 Copy these 4 animal shapes on a piece of poster board.

2 Carefully cut them out. Add all the details on both sides of the animal. Color the hearts and diamonds red. Color the spades and clubs black.

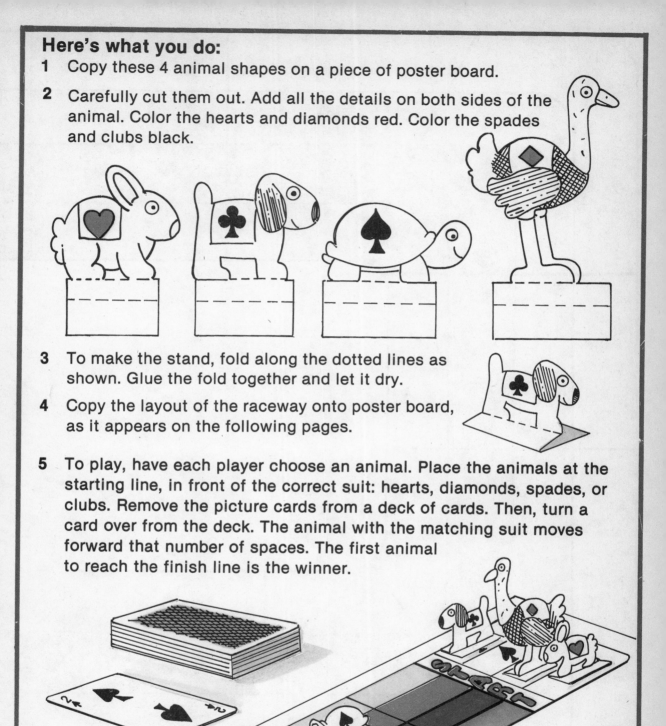

3 To make the stand, fold along the dotted lines as shown. Glue the fold together and let it dry.

4 Copy the layout of the raceway onto poster board, as it appears on the following pages.

5 To play, have each player choose an animal. Place the animals at the starting line, in front of the correct suit: hearts, diamonds, spades, or clubs. Remove the picture cards from a deck of cards. Then, turn a card over from the deck. The animal with the matching suit moves forward that number of spaces. The first animal to reach the finish line is the winner.

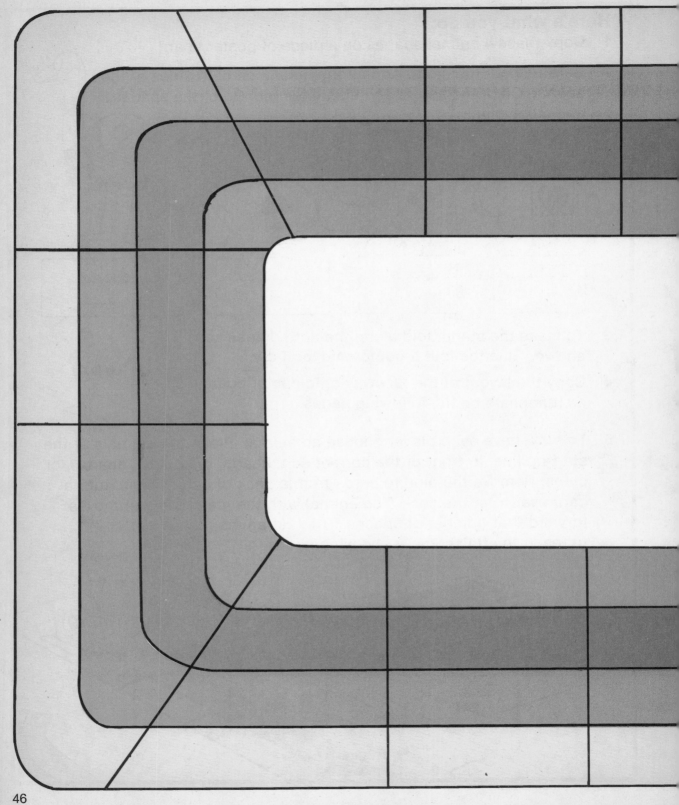

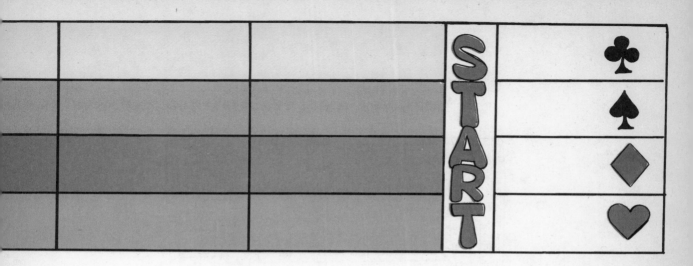

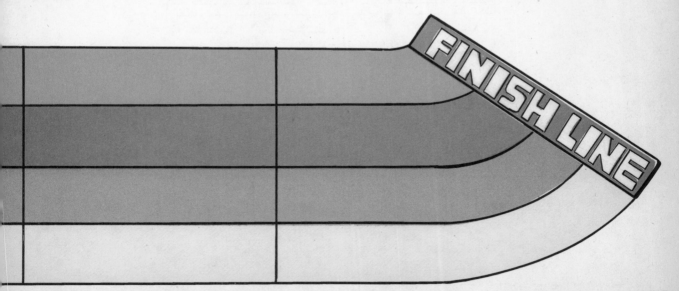